AMAZING ADVENTURES AT SEA

WRITTEN BY
ALEX HALL

All rights reserved.
Printed in India.

A catalogue record for this book is available from the British Library.

ISBN: 978-1-80505-603-4

Written by:
Alex Hall

Edited by:
Rebecca Phillips-Bartlett

Designed by:
Ker Ker Lee

©2024
BookLife Publishing Ltd.
King's Lynn, Norfolk
PE30 4LS, UK

All facts, statistics, web addresses and URLs in this book were verified as valid and accurate at time of writing. No responsibility for any changes to external websites or references can be accepted by either the author or publisher.

AN INTRODUCTION TO BOOKLIFE RAPID READERS...

Packed full of gripping topics and twisted tales, BookLife Rapid Readers are perfect for older children looking to propel their reading up to top speed. With three levels based on our planet's fastest animals, children will be able to find the perfect point from which to accelerate their reading journey. From the spooky to the silly, these roaring reads will turn every child at every reading level into a prolific page-turner!

CHEETAH
The fastest animals on land, cheetahs will be taking their first strides as they race to top speed.

MARLIN
The fastest animals under water, marlins will be blasting through their journey.

FALCON
The fastest animals in the air, falcons will be flying at top speed as they tear through the skies.

Contents

PAGE 4	Your Voyage at Sea
PAGE 6	Leif Erikson
PAGE 10	Zheng He
PAGE 12	Ferdinand Magellan
PAGE 16	Jeanne Baret
PAGE 18	Bungaree
PAGE 22	Fabian Gottlieb von Bellingshausen
PAGE 24	William Beebe
PAGE 26	Dr Sylvia Earle
PAGE 30	Where Will Your Voyage at Sea Take You?
PAGE 31	Glossary
PAGE 32	Index

Words that look like THIS are explained in the glossary on page 31.

Your Voyage at Sea

Ahoy! We are about to follow in the footsteps of the greatest ocean explorers.

Most of our planet is covered by water. Many great explorers have travelled these oceans in the hopes of discovering something interesting.

There is still so much left to explore. Would you like to begin your voyage at sea?

Then what are you waiting for? It is time to get your sea legs on and let the adventure begin.

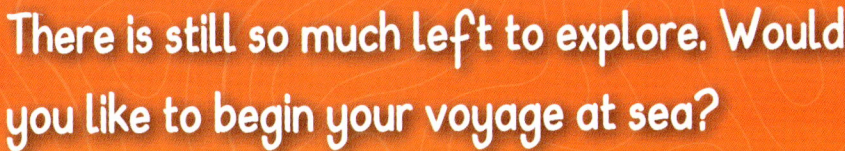

Leif Erikson

Around 970-1020

Our journey begins in Iceland, where a Viking named Leif Erikson was born.

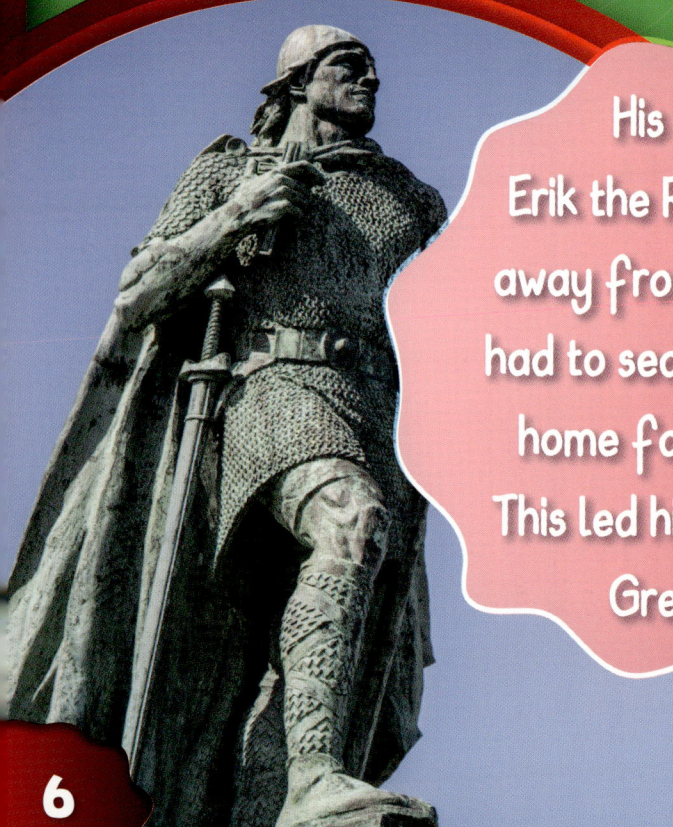

His father, Erik the Red, was sent away from Iceland and had to search for a new home for his family. This led him to discover Greenland.

Just like his father, Erikson set sail and explored. He became the first European to settle in North America.

Erikson named this land Vinland, otherwise known as 'the land of wine' because there were so many grapes for making wine.

In 1964, the President of the United States decided the 9th of October would become Leif Erikson Day.

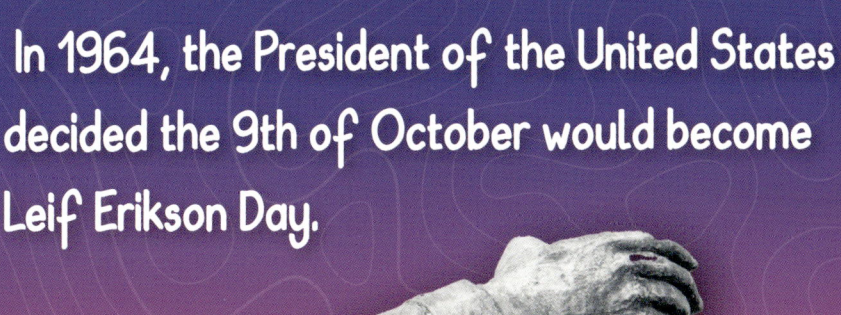

Leif Erikson's <u>legacy</u> lives on to this day. It was his curiosity that led to his success.

ZHENG HE

1371–Around 1433

Here we are in China. This is where Zheng He was born.

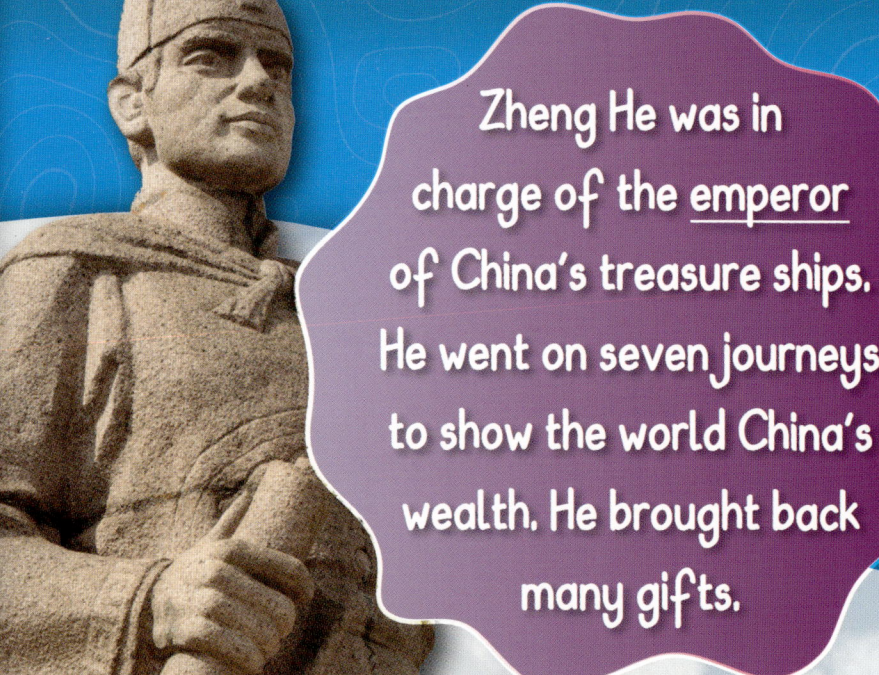

Zheng He was in charge of the emperor of China's treasure ships. He went on seven journeys to show the world China's wealth. He brought back many gifts.

Zheng He even travelled as far as East Africa. In Africa, he got a giraffe as a gift for the emperor. Many people thought it was a magical animal.

Zheng He helped China trade with many other countries.

Ferdinand Magellan

1480–1521

The next trip is going to be a long one.

When Ferdinand Magellan was born, no one had ever sailed around the world. Magellan wanted to try for himself. Magellan was born in Portugal, but his voyage began in Spain.

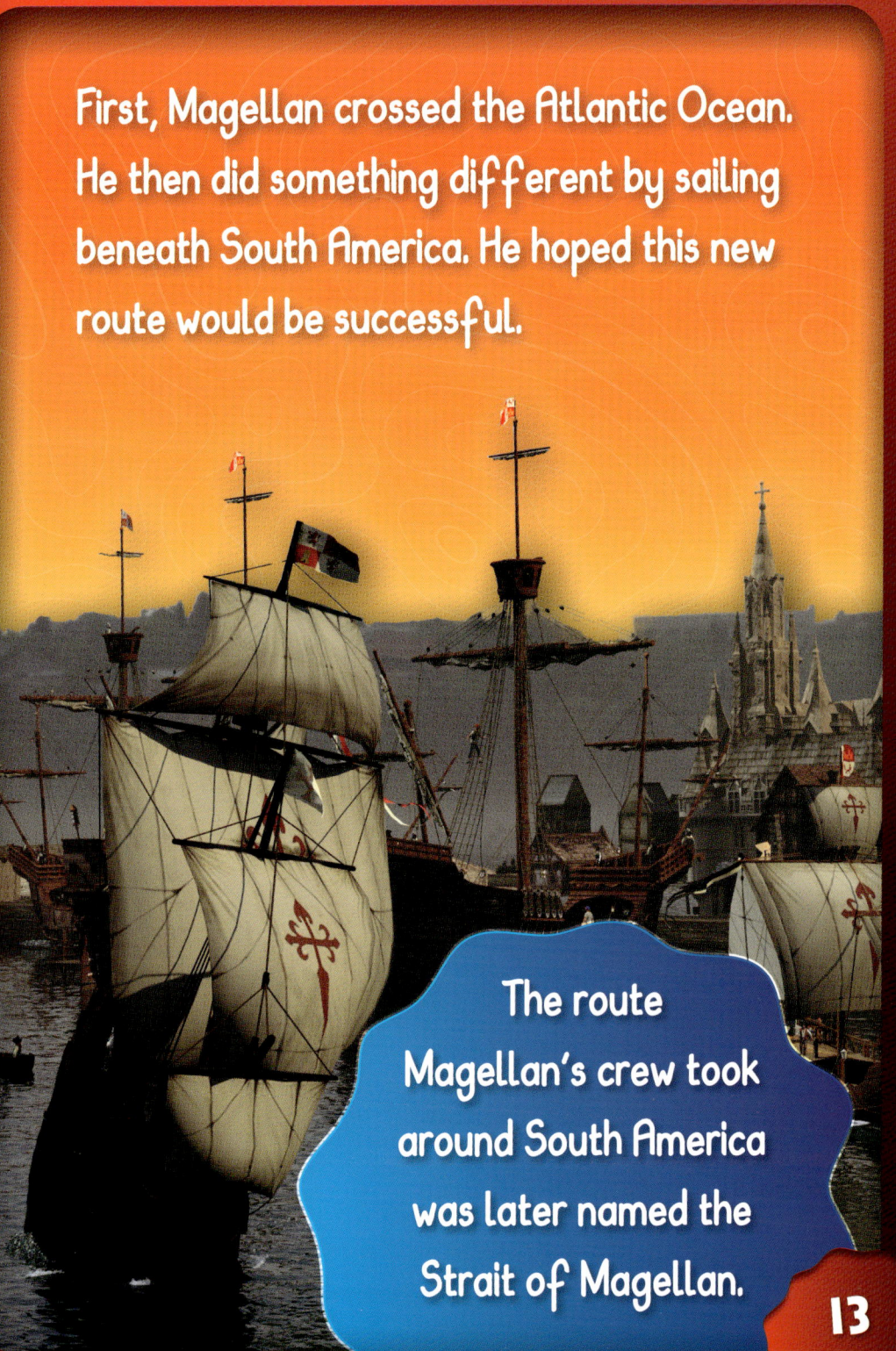

First, Magellan crossed the Atlantic Ocean. He then did something different by sailing beneath South America. He hoped this new route would be successful.

The route Magellan's crew took around South America was later named the Strait of Magellan.

After 99 days at sea, Magellan and his crew finally found land. Magellan died when he landed in the Philippines.

The navigator, Juan Sebastián Elcano, took over the expedition and completed the voyage.

JUAN SEBASTIÁN ELCANO

The crew were the first people to sail around the world in one trip.

Magellan, Elcano and their crew proved that Earth is round. This gave people a new understanding of how the world works.

Jeanne Baret

1740-1807

We are going around the world again to see how a French woman called Jeanne Baret made history.

Jeanne Baret's partner joined a trip to sail around the world. Baret was not allowed to join because she was a woman.

Baret <u>disguised</u> herself as a man to join the trip. She studied many flowers on the journey. She even had a flower named after her.

Thanks to Baret's determination, she became the first woman to sail around the world.

BUNGAREE

1775–1830

Get ready to go down under because the next stop is Australia. It is where <u>Aboriginal</u> Australian Bungaree was born.

Bungaree was a friendly and intelligent man. Many powerful people liked him because of this.

Matthew Flinders was an English officer. Flinders liked how friendly Bungaree was, so he gave Bungaree a job on his ship.

MATTHEW FLINDERS

Bungaree talked to other Aboriginal people without knowing their language. He used hand signs to show he was peaceful.

Bungaree travelled with Flinders on his longest voyage yet. Bungaree was the only person born in Australia on the ship.

Bungaree became the first Aboriginal Australian to sail around all of Australia.

Bungaree helped to map out the coastline of his home country. These changes are still used on maps today.

Bungaree's kindness and friendliness gave him many opportunities as he travelled. He is now remembered as a great explorer.

Fabian Gottlieb von Bellingshausen

1778–1852

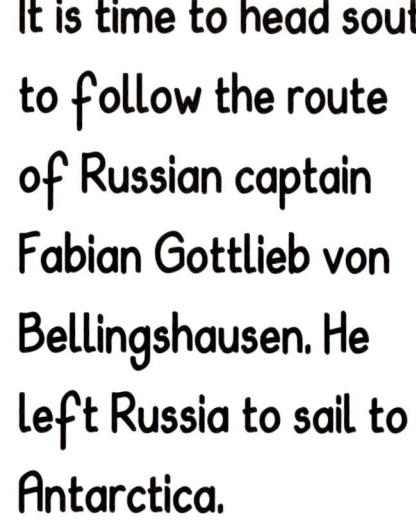

It is time to head south to follow the route of Russian captain Fabian Gottlieb von Bellingshausen. He left Russia to sail to Antarctica.

Many others tried to take the journey to Antarctica, but the trip was too dangerous.

Bellingshausen's journey took over two years. There were some bad storms that were very difficult to get through. Bellingshausen did not give up when things got tough.

Bellingshausen is now remembered as the first person to see Antarctica.

William Beebe

1877–1962

What about underwater adventures? American scientist William Beebe thought the same when he studied underwater life.

Beebe and a man called Otis Barton invented the bathysphere. This was a metal ball that allowed them to travel deep underwater.

The bathysphere was dangerous, but Beebe took the risk to learn more about underwater life.

Beebe's underwater adventures would not have succeeded without the clever men and women in his team.

THE BATHYSPHERE

Dr Sylvia Earle

1935

We are staying under the water for this last sea hero. Dr Sylvia Earle is an American oceanographer and explorer.

An oceanographer is a scientist who learns about oceans and the life in them. Earle has spent over 1,000 hours diving.

Earle set a record for diving 381 metres under the Pacific Ocean and walking around on the ocean floor.

Earle became the first woman to go 30 metres under the ocean.

EARLE WAS FOUR MONTHS PREGNANT AT THE TIME!

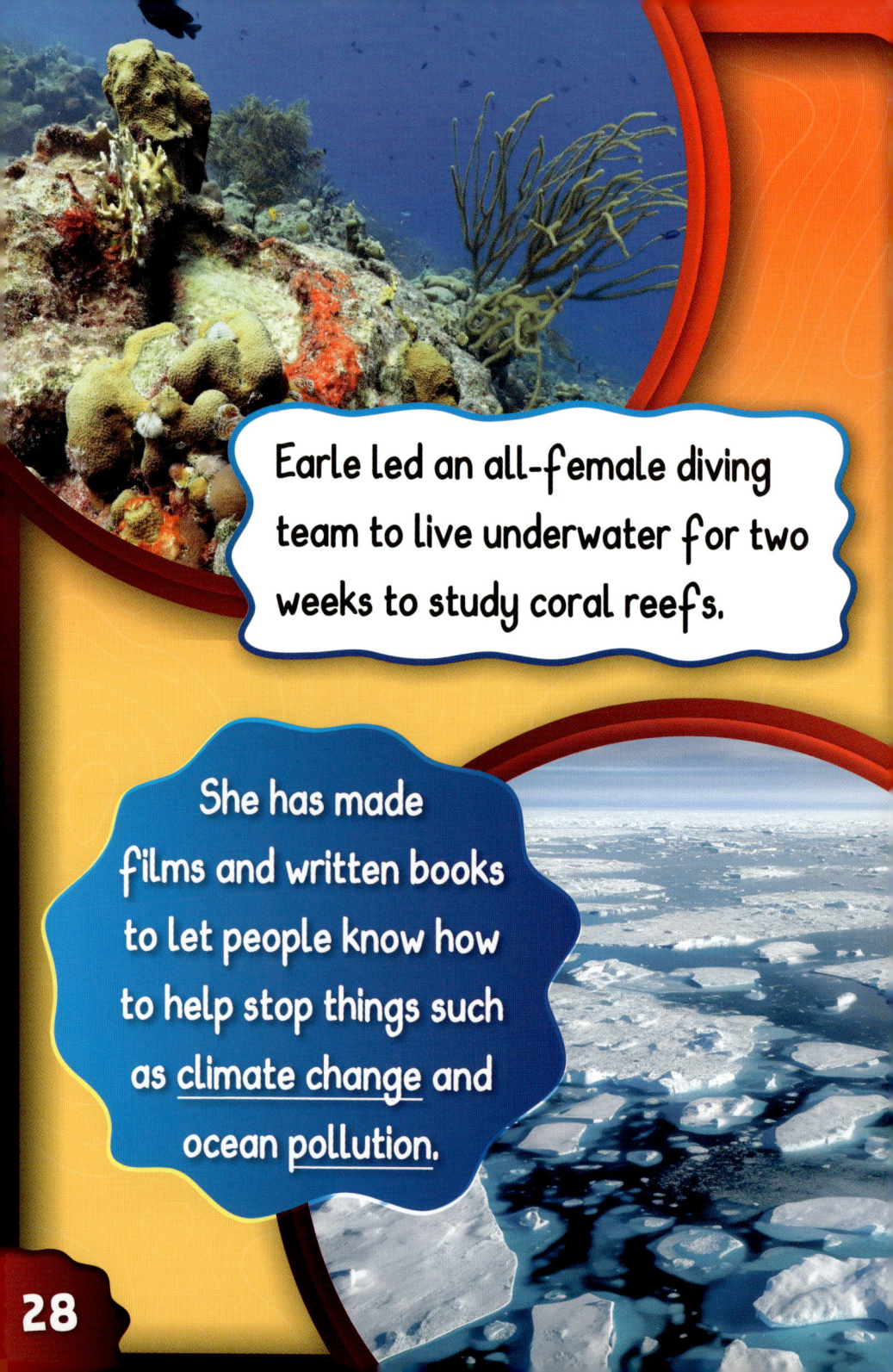

Earle led an all-female diving team to live underwater for two weeks to study coral reefs.

She has made films and written books to let people know how to help stop things such as climate change and ocean pollution.

Earle set up an organisation that tries to protect ocean life from climate change and pollution.

Dr Sylvia Earle pushed herself to her full potential. She is still adding to her legacy today.

DR SYLVIA EARLE

Where Will Your Voyage at Sea Take You?

That was a long journey! Sailing all over the world is impressive. You should be so proud that you did it.

Will you be leading the next voyage at sea? Maybe one day people will talk about your great adventures!

GLOSSARY

Aboriginal	to do with the first people to ever live in a place, such as the native people of Australia
climate change	a change in the typical weather or temperature of a large area
disguised	used an outfit that hides what someone really looks like
emperor	a person who rules over lots of land and people
expedition	a journey for a specific purpose
legacy	the lasting memory of a person or something handed down from one generation to the next
pollution	harmful and poisonous things being added to a place

INDEX

Antarctica 22–23

bathyspheres 24–25

flowers 17

gifts 10–11

Greenland 6, 8

languages 19

life 24–26, 29

maps 21

routes 13, 22

ships 10, 19–20

treasure 10

Vikings 6

Photo Credits – Images are courtesy of Shutterstock.com. With thanks to Getty Images, Thinkstock Photo and iStockphoto.
Recurring images – Elena Pimukova, Svetolk, Dancake. Cover – Ravelios, Regien Paassen. 4–5 – Alvov, Jenna Aloia Photography. 6–7 – Ivan Marc. 8–9 – Sharon Mollerus, CC BY 2.0 <https://creativecommons.org/licenses/by/2.0>, via Wikimedia Commons, Riptaid. 10–11 – beibaoke, Kosov vladimir 09071967, CC BY-SA 4.0 <https://creativecommons.org/licenses/by-sa/4.0>, via Wikimedia Commons. 12–13 – Jaime Grech Santos. 14–15 – 24K-Production, Prachaya Roekdeethaweesab. 16–17 – svic. 20–21 – Janaka Dharmasena. 22–23 – Olga Popova. 24–25 – Leo Wehrli, CC BY-SA 4.0 <https://creativecommons.org/licenses/by-sa/4.0>, via Wikimedia Commons. 28–29 – Mongkolchon Akesin, blue-sea.cz, Osipov Art. 30 – VladyslaV Travel photo.